"A STUDY FOR TEENS ON WHAT GOD SAYS ABOUT MONEY"

Dave Ramsey's Publishing Department
The Lampo Group, Inc. | 1749 Mallory Lane, Ste. 100 | Brentwood, TN 37027

Written by:
Marcie Kindred

Contributing Writer:
Bryan Currie

Edited by:
Daniel Chunn, Rachel DeMass, Brenee Dihigo, Michael Edwards,
Allen Harris, Michelle Kobosky, Simon Lawrence, David Taylor,
Matt Woodburn, and Neal Webb

Cover and Design:
Scott Lee Designs

For more information, please contact:
The Lampo Group, Inc. Toll Free at 888.227.3223 Fax 615.550.6220
E-mail:generationchange@daveramsey.com
www.daveramsey.com

TABLE OF CONTENTS

GENERATION CHANGE PLEDGE

I KNOW HOW MONEY REALLY WORKS, HOW GOD VIEWS MONEY, AND HOW TO BE RESPONSIBLE WITH WHAT I HAVE BEEN GIVEN.

> I **KNOW** I HAVE VALUE THROUGH GOD'S EYES
> I **KNOW** THAT NO AMOUNT OF "STUFF" CAN CHANGE MY SELF-WORTH
> I **KNOW** THE DANGERS OF DEBT, FROM CREDIT CARDS TO CAR PAYMENTS
> I **KNOW** WHY AND HOW TO SAVE MONEY AND PAY CASH FOR WHAT I WANT
> AND I **WILL** LIVE A LIFESTYLE OF GENEROUS GIVING THAT CAN CHANGE THE WORLD AROUND ME FOREVER!

I AM A GENERATION OF CHANGE! _____

SIGNATURE

Dave Ramsey, a personal money management expert, is an extremely popular national radio personality and author of the New York Times best-sellers The Total Money Makeover, Financial Peace and More Than Enough. Ramsey knows first-hand what financial peace means in his own life – living a true rags-to-riches-to-rags-to-riches story. By age twenty-six he had established a four-million-dollar real estate portfolio, only to lose it by age thirty. He has since rebuilt his financial life and now devotes himself full-time to helping ordinary people understand the forces behind their financial distress and how to set things right – financially, emotionally and spiritually. He is especially passionate about helping teenagers learn about money early so they can avoid debt and get off to a great start financially.

Rachel Ramsey was shown at a very young age how to follow in her parents' footsteps. Rachel's Mom and Dad, Dave and Sharon, intentionally taught their three children the four main areas of money: working, saving, spending, and giving. Unlike other kids, she was not given an allowance. Instead she was paid a commission, teaching that life will not make allowances for you, but it will pay you what you earn. By the time she was in her teenage years Rachel was ready to handle an entire household budget. She has been speaking to audiences of 3,000 to 10,000 since age 16 and is a graduate of Dale Carnegie Training. Now she is attending college where she successfully manages her own finances while majoring in Communication Studies.

DAVE RAMSEY'S
GENERATION
CHANGE

VALUE OF YOU

The Value of You - Snapshot

THE BIG PICTURE

The objective of Session 1, "The Value of You," is to understand that money isn't good or bad on its own—it takes on your character. Your character and identity aren't based on the things around you or on the stuff you buy, but on the soul within you. You are valuable because Christ values you!

CASHING IN: APPLICATION

There are many distractions along life's way, but the true hunt for happiness is an inward journey that begins and ends with Jesus.

TRUTH BE TOLD: THE BOTTOM LINE

You are valued. There is nothing you can do that will separate you from God's love or make Him love you any more or less than He already does.

The Value of You - Video Notes
Please fill in the blank.

1. Setting _____ helps you achieve your highest potential.

2. _____ to live like no one else.

3. _____ where you are going.

4. **Romans 5:3-5**
_____ in our sufferings…
Suffering produces perseverance…
Perseverance character, and character _____ …

5. **1 Timothy 6:10**
For the _____ of money is the root of all kinds of evil.

6. _____ is amoral.

7. God cares how you _____ what you have not how much you have.

Romans 4:7-8
Blessed are they whose transgressions are forgiven, whose sins are covered. ⁸Blessed is the man whose sin the Lord will never count against him.

John 10:10
The thief comes only to steal and kill and destroy; I have come that they may have life, and have it to the full.

SESSION 1

VALUE OF YOU

DISCUSSION QUESTIONS

1. When adults look at you and your friends, what do you think they see? What would they think is important to you? Are their thoughts of you true?

2. Do you ever hide behind your "stuff" so that other people—or God—won't be able to see the real you? How would your friendships change if all your "stuff" was taken out of the picture?

3. What is it about us that Jesus values so much? Does He care more about what we have or who we are? At the end of the day, how important are our possessions?

1. **Psalm 139:13-16** - God had a relationship with you before you were even born and He has given you a unique job to do. What do you think that could be?

2. **Matthew 10:29-31** - You are much more important to God than you realize. God knows every detail about you, right down to the hairs on your head. How is this comforting to you? In what ways does it scare you a little bit?

3. **Genesis 1:26-27**- God isn't sitting in a big chair in heaven, just waiting for you to mess up so He can throw a lightning bolt your way. He loves you! He created you in HIS image! God is never too busy to listen to you when you call on Him. Why, then, don't we always feel comfortable going to Him with a question or concern?

4. **Romans 8:38-39** – No matter what you've done, Jesus still loves you just as much as He ever did. He sees through your sin to who you are, to who He made! Nothing can separate you from His love and nothing is too big for Him to forgive—NOTHING! Do you believe that?

MATERIALISM MAZE

MATERIALISM MAZE
An Interactive Experience Exploring The Need For Stuff

Instruction Sheet: please follow the instructions for each station below. Then, write down your response in the lines given.

STATION 1: WISHING WELL

Pick up a penny, make a wish, and place the coin in the "Wishing Bucket." Think about what you wished for. Why did you wish for that?

_____

_____

_____

_____

John 15:7-8

If you remain in me and my words remain in you, ask whatever you wish, and it will be given you. 8This is to my Father's glory, that you bear much fruit, showing yourselves to be my disciples.

1. If you were given an unlimited amount of wishes, what would they be? Write down your top three wishes.

_____

_____

_____

_____

2. Who would benefit the most from your wishes—you or some-one else?

_____

_____

_____

_____

STATION 2: BURIED TREASURE

Find some treasure (a coin) buried in sand. Keep the coin with you; you'll need it at the next station. If these coins were real gold, why would you want to look for them? What is the real treasure in you? If you could see yourself the way God sees you, how would that change you?

_____

_____

_____

_____

_____

_____

Proverbs 20:27

The lamp of the LORD searches the spirit of a man; it searches out his inmost being.

1. What would your friends list as your best qualities? What would you list?

Friends:

_____

_____

You:

_____

_____

2. What is one quality or ability that you wish you had? How would you use it?

_____

_____

_____

_____

Place your treasure coin from the previous station on the map where you live. We are part of the most materialistic society in the world. We get upset over little things like a dead cell phone battery while people in other parts of the world are facing war and poverty every day. What can you do to take the focus off of yourself and put it on others that are in need around you—maybe even in your own neighborhood?

_____

_____

_____

_____

_____

_____

Deuteronomy 15:11

There will always be poor people in the land. Therefore I command you to be openhanded toward your brothers and toward the poor and needy in your land.

1. List four things that you may take for granted that other people may not have at all.

_____

_____

_____

_____

2. True or False: It is not necessarily how much you have that counts; it is what you do with what you have that matters.

_____

_____

_____

_____

_____

STATION 4: THREE THINGS

Take three index cards. On each card, write down one thing that you own and enjoy (clothes, video game, etc.). Then, write down a dollar amount beside each item to represent what it is worth. If you could only keep one item, which would you choose? Why? Take the card you chose with you and throw the other two in the trash can.

_____

_____

Luke 12:15

Then he said to them, "Watch out! Be on your guard against all kinds of greed; a man's life does not consist in the abundance of his possessions."

1. What do your three items have in common?

_____

_____

_____

2. Why did you throw away the other two items?

_____

_____

_____

3. Why do people think their possessions make them powerful? In what ways is this true? How might this be a lie?

_____

_____

_____

Take a piece of candy from the bowl if your birthday is sometime between January and June. You're out of luck if your birthday is between July and December. Too Bad!

If you were able to take some candy, how do you feel about having some while others don't? Go ahead and enjoy your snack now . . . unless you want to leave it on the table beside the bowl for someone less fortunate to eat later.

If you are empty-handed, how do you feel about having to go without? If there's any candy on the table outside the dish, be grateful for someone else's generosity and enjoy a little snack. Or, you could leave it for someone else, too.

James 2:15-16

15 *Suppose a brother or sister is without clothes and daily food.* 16 *If one of you says to him, "Go, I wish you well; keep warm and well fed," but does nothing about his physical needs, what good is it?*

1. How did you feel if you were able to take a piece of candy?

_____

_____

2. How did you feel if you were not able to take a piece of candy?

_____

_____

3. If it applies to you, how does it make you feel to benefit from the generosity of others?

_____

_____

STATION 6: FAMILY FRAME

Think of all you have—clothes, shelter, food, cell phone, car, sports equipment, piano lessons, and so on. Have you ever considered how much it costs to meet your daily needs? Have you ever thanked the person who pays for all of this? What are some ways you can give back and help out?

_____

_____

_____

_____

2 Samuel 7:18

Then King David went in and sat before the LORD, and he said: "Who am I, O Sovereign LORD, and what is my family, that you have brought me this far?"

1. Are you thankful to God for your family? Why or why not?

_____

_____

_____

_____

2. Who are you close to in your family? Why?

_____

_____

_____

_____

3. Make a list of things your parents provide for you. Take a moment right now to write them a thank you letter with the cards provided. Please take the thank you cards with you as you go and give it to them the next time you see them.

_____

_____

_____

What are you known for? As minutes and hours turn into days and years, how will people remember you? Will they know you for who you are or for all the stuff you have around you? Take a moment and ask God what He wants you to be today, tomorrow and throughout the rest of your life.

_____

_____

_____

_____

_____

_____

Psalm 112:6

A righteous man will be remembered forever.

1. In the next few moments, write down the words that you would want your grandkids to say about you.

_____

_____

_____

_____

_____

2. Every single one of us has the capacity to change. Is there any negative thing in your life that you need to change now in order for you to become the person you want to be in the future?

_____

_____

_____

_____

_____

STATION 8: CROSS CONFESSIONS

What did you wish for back at "The Wishing Well" station? Was it a "thing" or something intangible? There is nothing wrong with having nice things as long as the things you have don't control or consume you.

_____

_____

_____

Take out the index card with your favorite item written on it and look at it for a moment. How does this item compare to the security we have in Christ? Does it look small and almost silly in comparison? If so, fold the card and lay it down by the cross as an act of thankfulness for all that Christ has provided and done for you.

_____

_____

_____

_____

Ephesians 5:20

Always [give] thanks to God the Father for everything, in the name of our Lord Jesus Christ.

List two ways in which you can thank God today for all He has done for you.

1. _____

_____

_____

2. _____

_____

_____

Take a wipe and clean your hands. Think about all your hands have reached for in the past. Some things brought joy, others pain, and still others probably left you wanting something more. As you clean your hands, clean your mind and challenge yourself to stop reaching out for things for the wrong reasons and start reaching out to God. When you do, you'll discover a new you that is free from the bondage of stuff!

Jeremiah 6:16

This is what the LORD says: "Stand at the crossroads and look; ask for the ancient paths, ask where the good way is, and walk in it, and you will find rest for your souls."

1. What are the idols in your life that compete against God for your time and attention?

   _____

   _____

   _____

2. Are there any "friends" in your life that only like you because of what you have or can offer them? Are they really a friend?

   _____

   _____

   _____

3. Look back on your life. Do you like what you see or who you have become? Why or why not? If not, what can you do differently from this point forward?

   _____

   _____

   _____

   _____

   _____

STATION 10: FACE IN THE MIRROR

Look at yourself. Admire the person in the mirror as someone made in God's image. You are His awesome creation—and He does good work! The world may tell you that you need to look like this or have that for people to like you, but you are already complete! Nothing more is needed to beautify God's masterpiece in you!

How can you live in a way that will show respect for God's handiwork? Will your family be able to see a change in you? Will your friends? Please take a moment to anonymously write your thoughts, feelings, and prayers down and place it in the plate as an offering to God.

Genesis 1:27
So God created man in his own image, in the image of God he created him; male and female he created them.

Psalm 139:14
I praise you because I am fearfully and wonderfully made; your works are wonderful, I know that full well.

1. How do you reflect God's image?

_____

_____

_____

2. Identify five ways in which you are wonderfully made.

_____

_____

_____

3. Share positive comments with a friend or a family member this week on how God has made them in His image and that they are wonderfully made!

MATERIALISM MAZE

SESSION 2
MATERIALISM MAYHEM

Materialism Mayhem - Snapshot

THE BIG PICTURE
The objective of Session 2, "Materialism Mayhem," is to unveil this world's unhealthy spending habits. We often buy things that we cannot afford on credit, thinking we'll just pay for it later. Many times, later never comes. This session will help you learn to plan your purchases wisely and create an age-appropriate budget. You will come away with an empowerment over money and wisdom to handle money God's way.

CASHING IN: APPLICATION
We live in the most marketed-to culture in the history of the world. Companies aggressively compete for our attention—and our dollars. But a good manager of God's resources always has a plan for where, when, and how to spend money.

TRUTH BE TOLD: THE BOTTOM LINE
Handling money God's way is much different than how the world tells you to spend, spend, spend. Honestly, it may even be different than the way your family uses money. Credit cards and other forms of debt are simply ways for people to spend money they don't have on stuff they usually don't need. The bottom line is this: If you can't pay for it, you aren't ready to buy it.

Materialism Mayhem – Video Notes
Please fill in the blank.

Romans 13:7
Give everyone what you owe him: If you owe taxes, pay taxes; if revenue, then revenue; if respect, then respect; if honor, then honor.

1. **Proverbs 22:7**
   The borrower is _____ to the lender.

2. We buy stuff with money we don't have, to _____ people we don't really like.

3. Don't sign up for _____ .

4. Credit card companies market directly to _____ .

5. Adults are not defined by what they have but how they _____ .

6. _____ credit card marketing schemes.

7. Your most powerful wealth building tool is your _____ .

8 . Don't allow _____ to control your life.

9. **Luke 14:28-30**
   Suppose one of you wants to build a tower. Will he not first sit down and estimate the _____ ...

10. Have a _____ and write it down on paper, on purpose, before the month begins.

11. Plan how you _____ .

John 3:16
"For God so loved the world that he gave his one and only Son, that whoever believes in him shall not perish but have eternal life."

MATERIALISM MAYHEM

DISCUSSION QUESTIONS

1. Have you ever made a big purchase without really planning for it? That's called an "impulse purchase." What are some things that you buy on impulse and what are some things you plan for? When is it smart to think before you make a purchase?

2. Is money a tool? How important is it to have the right tool for the right job?

3. Dave said that if debt is normal, we should be weird. What did he mean by that? Is it good to be weird? What will weird bring you?

SESSION 2

MATERIALISM MAYHEM

SCRIPTURE QUESTIONS

1. **Matthew 6:19-34** - This is one of the most detailed Scripture passages that warns against the need for stuff. We can draw a lot of questions out of this passage. Is it wrong to have nice things? How can you use the things you have for God's glory? What is the difference between storing up treasure here on earth as opposed to heaven? Why can't you serve two masters? Who would you say is your master? If God takes care of birds and flowers, why do you sometimes worry that He won't take care of you?

2. **Philippians 4:11-13** – Here Paul discusses the secret of contentment, whether he is rich or poor. What do you think is the basis for Paul's contentment?

YOUTH SAMPLE SPENDING SHEET

Item	Cost of item	Cost each day	Cost each week	Cost each month
Lunch	$5	$5	$5 x 5 days = $25	$25 x 4 weeks = $100
Bus/metro pass	$2.50	N/A	$2.50 x 3 =$7.50	$7.50 x 4 weeks = $30
Cell phone	N/A	N/A	N/A	$30 monthly bill
Gas (1 tank full)	$50 every 2 weeks	N/A	$25	$50 x 2 fill ups =$100
Movie and dinner w/ friends	N/A	N/A	$15	$15 x 4 weeks = $60
Clothes	N/A	N/A	N/A	$75
Guitar lessons	$40 a lesson	N/A	$40	$40 x 4 weeks =$160
(want) computer	$1,000	N/A	N/A	$1000/10 months = $100
(want) car	$4,000	N/A	N/A	$4,000/20 months = $200
(want) springbreak w/plane ticket	$900	$180 x 5 days = $900	N/A	$900/4 months = $225

TOTAL for the Month = $1,080.00

A Zero based budget is when your income minus your expenses equals ZERO.

NOTE: This sheet only gives examples of spending. A real budget needs to include a plan for giving and long term savings as well.

REAL WORLD SAMPLE BUDGET based on $30,000

Item	Cost of item	Cost each day	Cost each week	Cost each month
Giving	N/A	N/A	N/A	$250
Possible savings	N/A	N/A	N/A	$515
Possible debt	$2,200	N/A	N/A	$110
Rent	N/A	N/A	N/A	$625
Utilities *(gas, water, electric, etc.)*	N/A	N/A	N/A	$200
Gas, car repair, and insurance	N/A	N/A	N/A	$180
Health insurance *(excluding dental & vision)*	N/A	N/A	N/A	$110
Food	N/A	$10	$70	$280
Restaurant/ entertainment	N/A	N/A	$30	$120
Phone	N/A	N/A	N/A	$60
Clothes	N/A	N/A	N/A	$50

TOTAL for the Month = $2,500.00

***Note: Car is paid for and there are no medical expenses

BLANK BUDGET WORKSHEET

Item	Cost of the item	Cost each day	Cost each week	Cost each month

TOTAL for the Month =

When Budgets Don't Work

It is never too early to be responsibile with money. However, your budget will not work if:

- *You leave items out! Make sure you account for everything!*

- *You make it too complicated. If it becomes too hard to understand and implement, you probably will not stick to it!*

- *You do not actually do one.*

- *You do one but don't live on it. The reason you are doing a cash flow plan is to take control of your money and create accountability, right? If you don't follow it, what is the point of doing it?*

- *You don't write it down! Putting it on paper makes it real. Don't try to only keep it in your head!*

Saving up!

1. What you want to buy: _____

2. How much does it cost: _____

3. What is today's date: _____

4. When do you want it by: _____

5. How many months/weeks are there between now and when you want it: _____

Divide how much the item costs by the number of months/weeks and that is how much you need to budget to save on a monthly/weekly basis to buy your item.

EXAMPLE

What you want to buy: **Computer**

How much does it cost: **$1000**

What is today's date: **January 6th**

When do you want it by: **October (for College)**

How many months are there between now and when you want it: **10 months**

$1000 divided by 10 months = $100 a month is needed to save up to buy the computer in October.

Key Ingredients for Writing a Basic Resume:

Having a strong resume is important for getting that first interview. Below is key information to include in any resume. You can make it as fancy or as plain as you want, but the key is to make sure that all the pertinent information is there. You can refer to the sample on the following page for more information.

A good resume includes:

Name and contact information (address, phone number, email address, etc.)

Highest education completed (name and address of the school(s) and years that you attended; also a degree if applicable)

Previous experiences (includes past and present jobs and responsibilities held in any club or academic/social institution)

Special skills (anything that would set you apart from other applicants)

Special awards (don't brag, but be honest about any recognition you've received)

References (teachers, pastors, employers, etc.; be sure to get the individuals' permission before listing their contact information on a resume)

860 Valley Drive, Chicago, IL 37209
Phone 555.333.2222 • E-mail – gotme@internet.net

Joe C. Buck

Education
2003-2007 State College   Chicago, IL
Major: Business
GPA 3.1 (on 4.0 scale)

Professional experience
2/2005-present First Bank of Illinois   Chicago, IL
Branch Teller

11/2004-11/2005 The Money Bank Inc.   Scottsdale, IL
Sales, Customer Relations

12/2001-9/2004 Benny's Ice Cream Shop   Scottsdale, IL
Sales

10/1999-12/2001 The Sandwich Shop   Chicago, IL
Professional Sandwich Maker

Skills
• Computer Skills: Publisher / Word / Excel /Power Point
• Foreign Language: Spanish / French

Awards received
Teller Awards – Gold and Silver
State College Business Department Best of Class Award 2007
State College 2007 Alumni Award
National Honor Society
Who's Who of American Colleges and Universities
Boy's State Delegate and Senior Counselor 2002-present

References available upon request

MONEY MINDS

Money Minds – Snapshot

THE BIG PICTURE

The objective of Session 3, "Money Minds," is to understand the importance of a rainy day fund, how to make wise purchases using the power of cash, ways to handle money using the envelope system, tips for buying big-ticket items, and lastly, the advantages of saving money at an early age.

CASHING IN: APPLICATION

Mastering money takes work and patience. Like anything worthwhile, it will take time and energy—but the payout is huge!

TRUTH BE TOLD: THE BOTTOM LINE

There's no question about it: God gives us what we need when we need it. However, that doesn't mean we should just sit back and do nothing, expecting God to wait on us hand and foot. We must be obedient with prayerful planning, asking God to show us exactly what He wants us to do each step of the way. It is often through the planning and preparation that He pours out His richest blessings.

Money Minds – Video Notes

Please fill in the blank.

1. Cash is _____ because it's emotional.

2. _____ is emotional.

3. _____ makes you aware that you are spending.

4. The _____ _____ helps you keep track
   of what you've spent and where you've spent it.

5. The envelope system helps you control _____!

6. _____ is finite.

7. Your _____ _____ allows you to be
   prepared for an unexpected event.

8. You can be a _____ !

9. _____ % of millionaires are 1st generation rich.

10. The typical millionaire is just your _____ person
    that is smart with money.

11. **Proverbs 24:16**
    "For though a righteous man falls seven times, he _____
    again…"

Philippians 4:6

*Do not be anxious about anything, but in everything, by prayer
and petition, with thanksgiving, present your requests to God.*

1. People spend up to 12% more when they pay with credit cards instead of cash. Why do you think credit cards cause more impulsive spending? Is it easier to buy a $50 item with cash or on credit? Why or why not?

2. What is Murphy's Law? Is it true that bad things usually happen when you don't prepare for them? Discuss a time when you or someone you know did not prepare for something and "Murphy" visited.

3. Even if you don't become a pro athlete or sign a huge music contract, God has given you the ability to build a great amount of wealth over time. You could be a millionaire! Do you believe that? Why or why not?

MONEY MINDS

1. **Proverbs 1:1-7** -This passage is written by King Solomon, one of the wealthiest men of all time. He shows us that wisdom and discipline are essential for a successful life. What does it mean to "let the wise listen and add to their learning, and let the discerning get guidance?" How does this Scripture relate to what we have discovered so far about handling money? In what ways will you apply what you've learned?

2. **Proverbs 27:23-24** - Scripture calls us to know the condition of our wealth, seen in this passage as flocks and cattle. Why is it important to keep tabs on your money? How does this passage relate to the issue of saving an emergency fund?

3. **Genesis 41:46-49, 53-57** - What was Joseph's emergency plan? Was his plan focused on himself only, or was he concerned with other people, as well? What would have happened if Joseph had not planned ahead? What can you do to plan ahead?

4. **Luke 12:48** - What does this Scripture say about the relationship between being responsible and being given much? Look at your budget from last week. Is there room in it for giving?

THE BIG 5

5 HANDY QUESTIONS TO ASK WHEN MAKING THOSE BIG PURCHASES

1. Would you buy this product tomorrow if you were to wait overnight and had time to think about it? Would this give you time to research it more? Would this give you a chance to calm down and get over the "gotta-have-it-now" fever?

2. Is this item a need or a want? Carefully consider your motives in buying this item. Basic needs are food, clothing, transportation, and shelter. Everything else is a want. Remember stuff may buy short-term happiness, but true, lasting joy comes from within.

3. Do you understand the item? If you buy something just for bragging rights without really knowing how to use and enjoy it, is this a really good purchase?

4. Is there a better use for the money? Consider the opportunity cost. Once you buy an item, you can't do anything else with that money. In the long run, would it be better to save this amount for the future? Remember, time is your best friend when it comes to saving and building wealth!

5. Have you asked anybody their opinion? Seek wise counsel. Ask someone you trust and respect if they think buying that item is a good idea right now.

BEN & ARTHUR

Ben and Arthur both save $2,000 per year at 12%. Ben starts at age 19 and stops at age 26, so he only actually invested a total of $16,000. Arthur starts at age 27 and stops at age 65, so he invested a total of $78,000. By age 65, guess which brother came out ahead? ARTHUR NEVER CATCHES UP TO BEN!

	BEN		ARTHUR	
Age	Ben Invests	Ben Makes	Arthur Invests	Arthur Makes
19	$2,000	$2,240	$0	$0
20	$2,000	$4,749	$0	$0
21	$2,000	$7,558	$0	$0
22	$2,000	$10,706	$0	$0
23	$2,000	$14,230	$0	$0
24	$2,000	$18,178	$0	$0
25	$2,000	$22,599	$0	$0
26	$2,000	$27,551	$0	$0
27	$0	$30,857	$2,000	$2,240
28	$0	$34,560	$2,000	$4,749
29	$0	$38,708	$2,000	$7,558
30	$0	$43,352	$2,000	$10,706
31	$0	$48,554	$2,000	$14,230
32	$0	$54,381	$2,000	$18,178
33	$0	$60,907	$2,000	$22,599
34	$0	$68,216	$2,000	$27,551
35	$0	$76,802	$2,000	$33,097
36	$0	$85,570	$2,000	$39,309
37	$0	$95,383	$2,000	$46,266
38	$0	$107,339	$2,000	$54,058
39	$0	$120,220	$2,000	$62,785
40	$0	$134,646	$2,000	$72,559
41	$0	$150,804	$2,000	$83,506
42	$0	$168,900	$2,000	$95,767
43	$0	$189,168	$2,000	$109,499
44	$0	$211,869	$2,000	$124,879
45	$0	$237,293	$2,000	$142,104
46	$0	$265,768	$2,000	$161,396
47	$0	$297,660	$2,000	$183,004

48	$0	$333,379	$2,000	$207,204
49	$0	$373,385	$2,000	$234,308
50	$0	$418,191	$2,000	$264,665
51	$0	$468,374	$2,000	$298,665
52	$0	$524,579	$2,000	$336,745
53	$0	$587,528	$2,000	$379,394
54	$0	$658,032	$2,000	$427,161
55	$0	$736,995	$2,000	$480,660
56	$0	$825,435	$2,000	$540,579
57	$0	$924,487	$2,000	$607,688
58	$0	$1,035,425	$2,000	$682,851
59	$0	$1,159,676	$2,000	$767,033
60	$0	$1,298,837	$2,000	$861,317
61	$0	$1,454,698	$2,000	$966,915
62	$0	$1,629,261	$2,000	$1,085,185
63	$0	$1,824,773	$2,000	$1,217,647
64	$0	$2,043,746	$2,000	$1,366,005
65	$0	$2,288,996	$2,000	$1,532,166

. . . And he never caught up!

How much do you like your coffee drinks?

So, you don't think you can be a Ben and invest $2,000 a year. Well, let's try something else. Say you are 17 and enjoy meeting your friends at the local coffee shop once a week. While there, you spend an average of $5 on a beverage (which is about $20 a month). If you meet with them every week over next 10 years and stop at age 27, you will spend a total of $2,600 in coffee drinks. However, if you invest the same $5 a week and stop at age 27 (never putting in another dime), your money would grow to $236,604* by the time you turn 60! That's some expensive coffee, huh?

Based on 12% rate of return, which is what the market has almost averaged since the 1920's until now.

- Standard & Poor's 500 Composite Index (w/ reinvestment of dividends)

It is not necessarily how much you have that counts…it is what you do with what you have that really matters!

The Almost True Story of:
BEN, ARTHUR AND NED
(AKA - Brothers and their Bucks)

Cast: Ben, Arthur, Ned and "The Voice"

SCENE 1 — Ben, Arthur and Ned have just been paid for mowing the neighbor's grass. The following conversation happens as Ned splits the earnings with Ben and Arthur.

The Voice: In a modest neighborhood not too far from here live three boys—well, three brothers, really. Okay, if you want to get right down to it, they are triplets. In other words, Mom has had her hands full for the past 16 years! They don't have everything they want, but Mom makes sure they have everything they need. They are good boys that have (for the most part) been on the right side of the law. There was a toilet paper incident last summer, but that's another story.

Ben is the youngest by 12-minutes. He is rather shy, but great in sports. Arthur is what you call the middle child. How triplets can have a middle child we will never know, but he is the self-proclaimed middle of the three and likes it that way. Ned was born first, so that has officially made him the oldest. He is good in school, has a beautiful girlfriend named Lauren, and enjoys playing the guitar every night before he heads off to bed.

Today is Saturday and they just got paid by Mr. Spires, their neighbor, for mowing his grass.

(Ben, Arthur and Ned enter the room looking exhausted from a hard days work.)

Ned: Well boys, that's another Saturday of mowing Mr. Spires' grass!

Ben: I don't know how he did it for so long. Didn't he mow his own lawn until only a couple of years ago?

Arthur: Yeah, I think he's about 95 years old or something. I hope I'm in that good of shape when I'm his age!

Ned: Not only is he in good shape—he's loaded. I kind of feel guilty for taking his money. He pays us so well and when we ask him about it he always says…

Ned, Arthur and Ben: (smiling laughing and yelling at the same time): THREE MEN, THREE JOBS, THREE PAYCHECKS!!!!!

Arthur: I wonder how he got all that money to just give away like that?

Ned: I'm not sure. I think he was a history teacher at the old high school before they tore it down and built the new one.

Ben: That would explain all the maps lying around his house. He mentioned to me once that he invested money when he was young. Maybe that has something to do with all his loot.

Arthur: Huh?! (with a curious look on his face) Well, remind me to do that one day!

Ned takes three checks from his pocket that Mr. Spires gave him and hands them out.

Ned: (says in a joking manner) Here you go, guys. Don't spend it all in one place.

Ben: Hey, yea, what are you guys going to do with your loot?

Arthur: I've been wanting to buy some cool new clothes for a while now.

Ned: (says in a joking voice) Good idea! You need 'em! Maybe with your new clothes you won't scare all the girls away!

Arthur: (says mocking back) Ha, Ha, very funny. What are you
going to do with your money?

Ned: I am taking Lauren out to a nice dinner then to that chick flick
that she has been dying to see. How about you Ben, you're
kind of quiet. What are you going to do?

Ben: I'm not sure. I may save it!

Ned: Sure, man! Whatever floats your boat. Have fun going to the
bank!

Arthur: (says in a loving and joking way) Good idea, Ben! Then I
can borrow money from you someday!!!

SCENE 2 – Ben, Arthur and Ned are older now and have
met together to go fishing.

The Voice: Well, minutes turn into hours, hours turn into days,
days turn into weeks, weeks turn into years, and years...
well, you get it...bottom line—time passes. All three are
now married and have officially re-named themselves
"Dads with Diapers." They are great husbands and
wonderful dads. They all love their families and provide
for them as best as they can.

Ben is now a teacher and coach at the local high school. It doesn't
pay much, but he loves what he does and was just named teacher of
the year. Arthur is well...an author. He writes sports articles for the
paper and is occasionally asked to write for some of the bigger name
magazines. Ned's guitar practice has paid off and he just signed a
huge music contract. Life has been good for them. It is Saturday
afternoon. They meet at their childhood fishing hole and catch up
on life.

Ned, Ben and Arthur have fishing poles in their hands and are
attempting to fish. Ned is tangled in the fishing line while Ben and
Arthur look on.

Ned: C'mon guys—help a brother out!

Arthur: (comes over to help Ned) It is funny how you can make millions playing six strings and yet you tangle yourself to death with just one!

Ben: (says to Ned) Hey, I know you are doing well with your guitar gigs and everything. Do you really have millions?

Ned: Heck yes!

Arthur: (with a puzzled look) With all your "millions," why don't you at least buy a house or something—you know, invest some of that money before it slips through your fingers!

Ned: Ah, Arthur, now you sound like Mom! I am telling you, I travel all the time. Why would Lauren and I buy a house if we don't have time to live in it? Speaking of homes, are you enjoying your new place?

Arthur: I love it! Jenny and I never thought we would be able to build our own home. We built it on the golf course, no less. Ben even chipped in and helped out, didn't you Ben?

Ben: Yup! Those kitchen cabinets look good if I do say so myself. You know I think I may start a little wood-working business on the side doing that very thing. Hey, by the way, did you talk to our investment advisor, Charlie?

Arthur: I called him yesterday. We should be meeting sometime next week. Hey, Ned, you want to join us?

Ned: Join what?

Ben: Charlie helps us take care of our savings, you know, gives us the game plan for retirement. He is really good!

Ned: NO! I mean…no thank you! Hey, you guys do your thing… have fun. I just know that if I am saving it then I can't spend it. And if I can't spend it, I can't live the high life!

Arthur: Are you sure? There's no time like the present to start thinking of your future.

Ned: Future? I appreciate you two "mother hens" worrying about me but trust me, Lauren and I are doing great! I have never seen so much money in my life. In fact, let me buy you two tycoons dinner tonight, okay?

Ben: YOU BET!

Arthur: (with a huge laugh) Forget the pizza, Ben. Tonight, we're having steak!

SCENE 3 – Ben, Arthur and Ned are much older now. They are meeting at Arthur's house to play golf. Ned is running late and hasn't shown up yet.

The Voice: Well, minutes turn into hours, hours turn into days, days turn into weeks, weeks turn into years, and years...well, you get it...bottom line—more time passes. These guys are old!

Ben coaches the local team on occasion when he is in town. He started his cabinetry business, which doesn't bring in much money, but he enjoys it. Since we last saw Ben, he has developed a new hobby—travel. He and his family have been everywhere and just recently got back from Australia. He has watched a sports game in practically every country. He also started a savings account for each of his grandchildren. His oldest grandchild is in college and hasn't had to pay a dime of tuition out of his own pocket yet, thanks to Ben's saving habits and generosity.

Arthur is also doing well. He just recently published a novel. It is about three brothers...hum, sounds familiar! He and Jenny are still enjoying their home on the golf course and he has practiced his golf swing. He has entered local tournaments and usually places within the top-five.

Ned? Well, no one knows where Ned is at any given time. He and Lauren split up a while back. Ned said the divorce was mostly due to money. He didn't have any. He now owns a small home but keeps busy trying to pay off all the debt that he built up while "living the high life." It is Saturday afternoon. Ben and Arthur are on the golf course by Arthur's house. Ned hasn't shown up yet.

Arthur: (in a worried tone) Well, I'm sure he's okay. I guess he's just running late.

Ben: (trying to make Arthur laugh) It has got to be that old car of his. It probably broke down on the side of the road. I wouldn't worry though, I can just see some lady mechanic stop to help him out!

Arthur: Yup, I'm sure you're right! I just worry about him, you know?

Ben: Yes, I worry, too. I worry about you pulling your back out on all those moves you call a golf swing!

Arthur: (not amused) Funny…really funny! Sorry, I guess I should lighten up. It is a beautiful summer afternoon and we three old men are going to live it up today!

Ben: (as a confession) Live it up…you bet! I know I joke around a lot, but I worry about ole Ned, too. He has not been the same since Lauren left him.

Arthur: It is hard to spend your life with someone who only lives in the moment. Lauren told me once that credit companies would call all the time wanting money. The funny thing is they had the money to pay them—they just didn't.

Ben: I saw Lauren and the kids a couple of weeks ago. She is doing well and seems to be back on track. I guess money can put a wedge between the best of couples. You never know, do you?

(Both shake their heads in silence)

Arthur: Well, it has been a half hour now, should we go ahead and tee off? Oh, wait…

Arthur's phone rings. It is Ned. He answers it.

Arthur: (talking and pausing between comments as if talking to Ned on the other end. Hint: the longer the pause the more believable the conversation) Hey there stranger…
Yeah, we were just about to tee off. We can wait another ten minutes…
What?……………
At the grocery store…………………..
They won't let you off………………..
Well you do know your way around the canned food aisle!…..
Yup…………..
I will……….……
Yes, he is here too………………..
Just a second…….
Here he is…
(hands Ben the phone)

Ben: (now talking to Ned on the phone)
Hey Bro!……….
Yes, I overheard……..
How about we meet up for dinner tonight?……..
Oh, you can't………
Aren't you too old to wait tables? Listen, let me just help you out. You don't even have to pay me back. You're way too old to be living like this!…
Ok………
I understand and I promise I won't ask again, I am sorry……….
I know………..
You bet buddy…..
Love you, too.
(Ben hangs up the phone and gives it back to Arthur.)

Arthur: Well, do you want me to tee off first?

Ben: Heck yes! You are going to wipe the floor with me. I need all the help I can get!

Arthur: All right old man, watch this…………………

THE END

⇗THE GIFT OF GIVING

The Gift of Giving – Snapshot

THE BIG PICTURE
The objective of Session 4, "The Gift of Giving," is to see the importance of giving. Financial blessing comes with an opportunity—and a responsibility—to bless others. A grateful heart is a giving heart. Being a good manager of God's money involves knowing how to share it. While the world says to hold on to your money with a clenched fist, Christ calls us to become givers with open hands.

CASHING IN: APPLICATION
God has blessed you abundantly, so don't worry about what God gives to others—focus on your own blessings! When your attention is focused on others who have more than you, you'll never be content and experience the joy that comes from a generous heart.

TRUTH BE TOLD: THE BOTTOM LINE
Giving is a spiritual act of worship. Remember, you're made in God's image . . . and God is a giver. So, when you give, you become more and more like Jesus.

The Gift of Giving – Video Notes
Please fill in the blank.

Mark 12:41-44

"Jesus sat down opposite the place where the offerings were put and watched the crowd putting their money into the temple treasury. Many rich people threw in large amounts. 42But a poor widow came and put in two very small copper coins, worth only a fraction of a penny. 43Calling his disciples to him, Jesus said, "I tell you the truth, this poor widow has put more into the treasury than all the others. 44They all gave out of their wealth; but she, out of her poverty, put in everything—all she had to live on."

1. Tithe: to give or pay a _____ .

2. **Numbers 18:25-26**
    "…You must present a tenth of that _____ as the Lord's offering."

3. **Genesis 1:27**
    "So God created man in his own _____ …"

4. **John 3:16**
"For God so loved the world that he _____ his one and only Son, that whoever believes in him shall not perish but have eternal life."

5. _____ is a part of your Christ-like pattern.

6. Tithes and offerings work the spiritual _____ of giving.

7. Every time you give, you become more _____ centered.

8. Others centered people are _____ to be around.

9. Giving allows you to prosper in your _____ .

10. When you're _____ with Christ, you're right where you're designed to be.

Matthew 6:21

For where your treasure is, there your heart will be also.

SESSION 4
THE GIFT OF GIVING
DISCUSSION QUESTIONS

1. As managers of God's money, we are also participants in God's work. How actively have you participated? In what ways might you need improvement?

2. Why was Jesus more impressed by the widow's small amount than the huge sums given by the wealthy people?

3. Dave says that giving makes you less selfish, more Christ-like, and a blessing to those you love. Describe the most generous person you know. Tell a story about someone who was generous towards you.

THE GIFT OF GIVING

SCRIPTURE QUESTIONS

1. **Psalm 24:1-6** - Everything belongs to God—everything. Understanding that point changes our whole perspective on giving, doesn't it? In what ways can you help your generation become a generation of giving?

2. **Leviticus 27:30-32** - We are reminded to tithe (give a tenth of our income) back to the Lord. When we tithe, we are constantly reminded of what God has done for us and how He has provided for our needs. In the Old Testament, God's people were instructed to give their very best—not their leftovers—as an offering to God. Why did God demand this? What was the lesson to be learned?

3. **Mark 10:17-24** - In this passage, Jesus meets a young man who loved his stuff more than he loved God. Be sure to notice that it was not his wealth that made him sinful; it was his attitude, his love for wealth and possessions. What are some things that you would find hard to give away? Are you as generous with others as you are with yourself?

4. **Matthew 6:1- 4** - Why is it important to give quietly? What do you usually think of people who publicly make a big deal of their giving?

5. **2 Corinthians 9:6- 8** - What does it mean to be a "cheerful giver?" Is it reasonable to expect someone to be excited about giving his or her money away? Why is your attitude important when you drop your money in the offering plate at church? In what way is giving considered an act of worship?

Dear Young'n,

Well, if you're reading this letter that means that your ole' Aunt Ira is outta this world and into the next. You always understood me and know first-hand that I had an adventurous spirit. The kids told me to settle down and find myself a good rocker to rest on. Well, I found a good rocker—you know, that electric guitar I found a few years ago, the one with the flames down the side. Please make sure your cousins get that thing—it was always a sweet guitar! Oh yes, please see that they also get that six-foot spear I kept in the kitchen for when we would barbeque out back. Tell them that it was given to me in Africa when I went on Safari a couple years ago. I would just hate for that thing to get lost when you sell this old bag of bricks of a house. I never knew why the kids told me to move into this "safe" neighborhood. I was never here! And it's not like I knew the neighbors—they were always gone making movies and such, oh well.

Anyway, you know I am not one for chit-chat. I love you, kid-o! Tell the neighbors I said good-bye and to have them watch out for the alligator in the pool when they sneak a swim. He only bites when he's hungry. As for you: along with the money I have already given you, please take the money in the enclosed envelope and give it away. You know I was always a big giver and I will expect no less from you. Don't worry about what I would do with it. It's up to you now. You can give it all in one place or divide it up as you see fit. I trust you! Well, I am off to pole vault the pearly gates. Take care and see you on the other side!

Love,

Aunt Ira

30 DAY DEVOTIONAL

2 Kings 22:1-6

1 *Josiah was eight years old when he became king, and he reigned in Jerusalem thirty-one years. His mother's name was Jedidah daughter of Adaiah; she was from Bozkath.* 2 *He did what was right in the eyes of the LORD and walked in all the ways of his father David, not turning aside to the right or to the left.*

3 *In the eighteenth year of his reign, King Josiah sent the secretary, Shaphan son of Azaliah, the son of Meshullam, to the temple of the LORD. He said:* 4 *"Go up to Hilkiah the high priest and have him get ready the money that has been brought into the temple of the LORD, which the doorkeepers have collected from the people.* 5 *Have them entrust it to the men appointed to supervise the work on the temple. And have these men pay the workers who repair the temple of the LORD -* 6 *the carpenters, the builders and the masons. Also have them purchase timber and dressed stone to repair the temple.*

1. Josiah was only eight years old when he became king, and yet look at how responsible he was with his nation's money. Why do you think he was so careful with his budget? What was his motivation?

_____

_____

2. The money that Josiah handled belonged to the Temple of the Lord. Where did it come from?

_____

_____

3. Do you follow Josiah's example? Even though you might be young, how do you use your money to do God's work? If you don't, what are some ways you could?

_____

_____

_____

Proverbs 17:15-17

15 *Acquitting the guilty and condemning the innocent—*
the LORD detests them both.
16 *Of what use is money in the hand of a fool,*
since he has no desire to get wisdom?
17 *A friend loves at all times,*
and a brother is born for adversity.

1. Make a list of four things you have bought recently on impulse. Compared to special gifts you've been given or things you have had to save and sacrifice to buy, how precious are these impulse items to you?

_____

_____

_____

_____

2. The proverb says, "of what use is money in the hand of a fool?" Television tabloids tell stories every day about wealthy celebrities and the millions they spend on extravagant houses, cars, and jewelry. In your opinion, is this foolish spending? If you think they could have spent more wisely, what would have been a better way to for them to have managed their money?

_____

_____

_____

_____

3. How can you be more wise with your money?

_____

_____

_____

_____

Ecclesiastes 5:10-11

10 *Whoever loves money never has money enough;*
   whoever loves wealth is never satisfied with his income.
   This too is meaningless.
11 *As goods increase,*
   so do those who consume them.
  And what benefit are they to the owner
   except to feast his eyes on them?

1. What is the difference in having a love of money and a respect for money?

_____

_____

_____

_____

_____

2. Explain the phrase "Whoever loves money never has money enough." Why is this phrase true?

_____

_____

_____

_____

_____

3. What are some things you can do to keep a wise perspective of money's real value and purpose?

_____

_____

_____

_____

_____

Ecclesiastes 7:11-12

11 *Wisdom, like an inheritance, is a good thing*
    and benefits those who see the sun.
12 *Wisdom is a shelter*
    as money is a shelter,
    but the advantage of knowledge is this:
    that wisdom preserves the life of its possessor.

1. How does wisdom "shelter" us? What does it "shelter" us from?

_____

_____

_____

_____

_____

2. How does money "shelter" us? What does it "shelter" us from?

_____

_____

_____

_____

3. As a teenager, you might not have much money to leave behind as an "inheritance" for your family if you were to die suddenly. What wisdom would you like to give to them instead? What has life taught you that you would like to leave as your inheritance? Which is more valuable, your cash or these insights?

_____

_____

_____

_____

_____

Isaiah 55:2

2 *Why spend money on what is not bread,*
   and your labor on what does not satisfy?
   Listen, listen to me, and eat what is good,
   and your soul will delight in the richest of fare.

1. What does it mean to "spend money on what is not bread"?

   _____

   _____

   _____

   _____

   _____

2. What are some things you have bought that you later regretted
   wasting your money? Why did you regret buying these
   things?

   _____

   _____

   _____

3. Isaiah asks why we would spend our labor on what does not
   satisfy. If you currently have a job, what do you get paid per
   hour? When you work for an afternoon, what do you earn?
   What is your time worth? Think about the last thing you
   bought that cost more than $20. Was this thing worth the
   amount of time it took you to earn that much money?

   _____

   _____

   _____

   _____

   _____

   _____

   _____

Luke 16:13-15

13 *"No servant can serve two masters. Either he will hate the one and love the other, or he will be devoted to the one and despise the other. You cannot serve both God and Money."* 14*The Pharisees, who loved money, heard all this and were sneering at Jesus.* 15*He said to them, "You are the ones who justify yourselves in the eyes of men, but God knows your hearts. What is highly valued among men is detestable in God's sight.*

1. Think about a time when you had to try to make several people happy who all wanted different things at the same time. How did it make you feel? Was it confusing? Exhausting? Why would trying to serve God while still being obsessed by money also make you feel this way?

_____

_____

2. The Bible says that as long as money is your master, you cannot serve God. Does this mean that rich people cannot serve God? Why or why not?

_____

_____

3. The Pharisees were "religious" men, yet they loved money. They pretended to love God, but their hearts told a different story. The Pharisees found Jesus' words offensive because they knew he was talking directly to them when he said you couldn't serve both God and money. If Jesus were to look at how you spend your money, the things you've bought, and the things you are still saving your money to buy, what do you think he would say to you?

_____

_____

_____

John 2:13-17

13*When it was almost time for the Jewish Passover, Jesus went up to Jerusalem.* 14*In the temple courts he found men selling cattle, sheep and doves, and others sitting at tables exchanging money.* 15*So he made a whip out of cords, and drove all from the temple area, both sheep and cattle; he scattered the coins of the money changers and overturned their tables.* 16*To those who sold doves he said, "Get these out of here! How dare you turn my Father's house into a market!"*
17*His disciples remembered that it is written: "Zeal for your house will consume me."*

1. In this story, why was Jesus mad? Do you think he over-reacted? Why or why not?

_____

_____

_____

2. The Temple was meant to be a holy place, set apart so that people could worship God without distraction. Sometimes, even at church, we let material things (technology, lights, sound, our friends, and even Christian events we want to attend) distract us from the church's purpose. What is your church's purpose? Why does it exist?

_____

_____

_____

3. What is the difference between selling items (books, music, DVD's, etc.) that help people in their Christian walk, and marketing random "Jesus merchandise" simply to make a quick buck? What do you think about the items that fill many Christian bookstores and concert concession tables? Are they appropriate? Why or why not?

_____

_____

_____

1 Timothy 3:2-4

2*Now the overseer must be above reproach, the husband of but one wife, temperate, self-controlled, respectable, hospitable, able to teach,* 3*not given to drunkenness, not violent but gentle, not quarrelsome, not a lover of money.* 4*He must manage his own family well and see that his children obey him with proper respect.*

1. An overseer is typically a manager, a boss, or someone in authority. Make a list of some people in your life who serve as a boss, a teacher, or as someone in authority. Do they have the qualities listed in 1 Timothy 3:2-4?

_____

_____

_____

2. Some of the people we are forced to follow really are bad leaders. Look at the people you listed in question #1. If the people you listed did not have these qualities described in 1 Timothy 3:2-4, did you think they were good leaders? Did you enjoy following them? What would have made them better leaders?

_____

_____

_____

3. People in power should be wise with money and not allow their love for money to consume the decisions they make. What is it about a judgment unclouded by money that enables good decision making? Could a person in power make better decisions if those decisions weren't solely based on money?

_____

_____

_____

1 Timothy 6:9-11

9*People who want to get rich fall into temptation and a trap and into many foolish and harmful desires that plunge men into ruin and destruction.* 10*For the love of money is a root of all kinds of evil. Some people, eager for money, have wandered from the faith and pierced themselves with many griefs.* 11*But you, man of God, flee from all this, and pursue righteousness, godliness, faith, love, endurance and gentleness.*

1. What job would you like to have one day? Why have you chosen this job?

_____

_____

_____

_____

2. Is it more important to choose a career based on how much money it earns, how happy it makes you, or on the amount of good it does? Rate these three criteria on a scale of 1-10 to show how important they are to you. Why did you assign each of them the number you did?

_____

_____

_____

_____

3. What is it about having money that makes some people happy? Is it the security of not worrying about having what you need? Is it being able to buy anything you want? Is it the status that money gives you? How is it possible for a poor person to be just as happy and satisfied with his/her life as a rich person?

_____

_____

_____

Hebrews 13:5-6

5*Keep your lives free from the love of money and be content
with what you have, because God has said,*
  "Never will I leave you;
    never will I forsake you." 6*So we say with confidence,*
  "The Lord is my helper; I will not be afraid.
  What can man do to me?"

1. Without saying anything generic like "clothes" or "CDs,"
   try to make a list of five specific presents you received
   for Christmas three years ago. If this is difficult, why is it
   difficult?

   _____

   _____

   _____

   _____

2. If you could make a list of any five things you would like for
   your parents to buy you for Christmas this year, what would
   you ask for? Do you think you will remember these gifts three
   years from now? Why or why not?

   _____

   _____

   _____

   _____

3. Money gets spent. It eventually runs out. Material
   possessions break, become outdated, and wear out.
   According to this scripture, what do we have that is more
   permanent than money or possessions?

   _____

   _____

   _____

   _____

James 4:13-17

13*Now listen, you who say, "Today or tomorrow we will go to this or that city, spend a year there, carry on business and make money." 14Why, you do not even know what will happen tomorrow. What is your life? You are a mist that appears for a little while and then vanishes. 15Instead, you ought to say, "If it is the Lord's will, we will live and do this or that." 16As it is, you boast and brag. All such boasting is evil. 17Anyone, then, who knows the good he ought to do and doesn't do it, sins.*

1. James seems to say in this scripture that it's wrong to make plans to go places, carry on business, and make money. What he really wants, however, is for us to gain the perspective that we "are a mist that appears for a little while and then vanishes." In other words, our plans for the future and our desire to make money aren't the most important things happening in the universe. Make a list of things that are more important than your bank account.

_____

_____

2. Rap stars, rock stars, and professional athletes are famous for flaunting their money. They wear flashy jewelry and drive expensive cars to show the world what they have. Why do you think James says that "all such boasting is evil?"

_____

_____

3. When you get your first job, you probably won't be making as much money as your parents make now. Your standard of living will go down. You will only be happy with your life if you can be satisfied with what you have and where you are in the moment. Why do you think this is hard for many people?

_____

_____

Psalm 37:16-21

16 *Better the little that the righteous have*
   than the wealth of many wicked;
17 *for the power of the wicked will be broken,*
   but the LORD upholds the righteous.
18 *The days of the blameless are known to the LORD,*
   and their inheritance will endure forever.
19 *In times of disaster they will not wither;*
   in days of famine they will enjoy plenty.
20 *But the wicked will perish:*
   The LORD's enemies will be like the beauty of the fields,
   they will vanish—vanish like smoke.
21 *The wicked borrow and do not repay,*
   but the righteous give generously;

1. Certain monks are not allowed to have any possessions?
    Why do you think that is?

_____

_____

_____

_____

2. Many lottery winners say that winning millions of dollars
   actually ruined their lives. Why do you think they say this?
   What is it about the money that makes them unhappy?

_____

_____

_____

_____

3. Why is it wicked to borrow and not repay (v.21)? How might
   this verse apply to the idea of creating credit card debt?

_____

_____

_____

Ecclesiastes 5:18-20

18 *Then I realized that it is good and proper for a man to eat and drink, and to find satisfaction in his toilsome labor under the sun during the few days of life God has given him—for this is his lot.* 19 *Moreover, when God gives any man wealth and possessions, and enables him to enjoy them, to accept his lot and be happy in his work—this is a gift of God.* 20 *He seldom reflects on the days of his life, because God keeps him occupied with gladness of heart.*

1. Some people wake up every morning (or leave school every afternoon), dreading that they have to go to work. Considering you will spend most of the next fifty years of your life in a job, it's important for you to enjoy what you do—to "accept [your] lot and be happy in [your] work." How does finding satisfaction in your job improve your quality of life?

---

2. The part-time job you have now is probably different from the career you will pursue after you graduate. What are some qualities a job must have in order for it to make you happy? (For example: I want to make things with my hands, I need to be creative, I want to help people, I like to work outside, I enjoy problems that involve numbers, etc.)

---

3. Solomon says that it's okay to have nice things and to enjoy them. He says that this is a gift of God. While you're enjoying your nice things, however, what can you do to keep from being obsessed with your possessions?

Luke 14:28-30

28 *"Suppose one of you wants to build a tower. Will he not first sit down and estimate the cost to see if he has enough money to complete it?* 29*For if he lays the foundation and is not able to finish it, everyone who sees it will ridicule him,* 30*saying, 'This fellow began to build and was not able to finish."*

1. Many people fall into credit card debt because their credit cards allow them to spend more money than they have. How might this scripture help these people?

   _____

   _____

   _____

   _____

2. Most people have a mental list of things that they would like to buy, but can't actually afford. Make a list of five things you would like to have but don't currently have enough money to pay for. Is it wrong to have this "wish list?"

   _____

   _____

   _____

3. Part of the problem with the tower in this scripture is that the man who started it was not able to finish it. Some things we buy naturally lead us to buy other things (for example, when you buy a car you must continue to buy gas, insurance, etc.) These purchases continue to drain our money. What are some things people buy that they might forget are like the tower and will continue to drain their resources?

   _____

   _____

   _____

   _____

Mark 12:14-17

14 *Is it right to pay taxes to Caesar or not?* 15*Should we pay or shouldn't we?"*

But Jesus knew their hypocrisy. "Why are you trying to trap me?" he asked. "Bring me a denarius and let me look at it." 16*They brought the coin, and he asked them, "Whose portrait is this? And whose inscription?"*

"Caesar's," they replied.

17*Then Jesus said to them, "Give to Caesar what is Caesar's and to God what is God's."*

1. Our government forces us to pay taxes. Some of these taxes come out of your pay check. You pay some of them every time you buy something at the store. What do you think the government spends our tax money on? Is it right that they should ask us to help pay for these goods and services?

2. The church also collects money. How do you think your church spends the money it collects? What does it buy? What does your church do with its money? Do you think it's right that your church should ask you to help pay for these goods and services?

3. Since God doesn't exactly have a bank account for you to deposit your money into, how can you "give to God what is God's?"

Matthew 25:14-30

14 *"Again, it will be like a man going on a journey, who called his servants and entrusted his property to them.* **15***To one he gave five talents of money, to another two talents, and to another one talent, each according to his ability. Then he went on his journey.* **16***The man who had received the five talents went at once and put his money to work and gained five more.* **17***So also, the one with the two talents gained two more.* **18***But the man who had received the one talent went off, dug a hole in the ground and hid his master's money.*

19 *"After a long time the master of those servants returned and settled accounts with them.* **20***The man who had received the five talents brought the other five. 'Master,' he said, 'you entrusted me with five talents. See, I have gained five more.'*

21 *"His master replied, 'Well done, good and faithful servant! You have been faithful with a few things; I will put you in charge of many things. Come and share your master's happiness!'*

22 *"The man with the two talents also came. 'Master,' he said, 'you entrusted me with two talents; see, I have gained two more.'*

23 *"His master replied, 'Well done, good and faithful servant! You have been faithful with a few things; I will put you in charge of many things. Come and share your master's happiness!'*

24 *"Then the man who had received the one talent came. 'Master,' he said, 'I knew that you are a hard man, harvesting where you have not sown and gathering where you have not scattered seed.* **25***So I was afraid and went out and hid your talent in the ground. See, here is what belongs to you.'*

26 *"His master replied, 'You wicked, lazy servant! So you knew that I harvest where I have not sown and gather where I have not scattered seed?* **27***Well then, you should have put my money*

*on deposit with the bankers, so that when I returned I would
have received it back with interest.*

28 *"'Take the talent from him and give it to the one who has the
ten talents. 29For everyone who has will be given more, and he
will have an abundance. Whoever does not have, even what he
has will be taken from him. 30And throw that worthless servant
outside, into the darkness, where there will be weeping and
gnashing of teeth.'"*

1. How did the servants in this story use their money to make
   more money? What can you do with your money that is more
   productive than simply spending it or keeping it in a checking
   account?

   _____

   _____

   _____

   _____

2. Why was it unwise for the third man to dig a hole and hide his
   money? What do you do with your money that is a modern
   equivalent to digging a hole in the ground to hide your money?

   _____

   _____

   _____

   _____

   _____

3. The unwise man gave many excuses for why he didn't act
   responsibly with his money. Why do you think people don't
   spend, save, or invest their money wisely?

   _____

   _____

   _____

   _____

   _____

Proverbs 13:11

Dishonest money dwindles away, but he who gathers money little by little makes it grow.

1. What does it mean for money to "dwindle away?"

_____

_____

_____

_____

_____

_____

2. Have you ever worked hard, earned some money, gotten a pay check, deposited the check in the bank, and then suddenly run out of cash, wondering where it all went? Think through the things you've bought during the last week. What are some of the small purchases that seem to drain money out of your pocket?

_____

_____

_____

_____

_____

_____

3. How can you gather money "little by little" in order to make it grow?

_____

_____

_____

_____

_____

Genesis 47:13-15

13 *There was no food, however, in the whole region because the famine was severe; both Egypt and Canaan wasted away because of the famine.* 14 *Joseph collected all the money that was to be found in Egypt and Canaan in payment for the grain they were buying, and he brought it to Pharaoh's palace.* 15 *When the money of the people of Egypt and Canaan was gone, all Egypt came to Joseph and said, "Give us food. Why should we die before your eyes? Our money is used up."*

1. When Joseph collected the people's money and brought it to Pharaoh's palace, what do you think he spent it on? Do you think he used the money to decorate the palace, or did he save it for a greater purpose? Read again what the people of Egypt said to Joseph. What do you think Joseph spent the money on?

_____

_____

_____

2. What can you learn from Joseph about how you should manage your money?

_____

_____

3. Joseph was not only wise with his own money, but with other people's as well. At Christmas, on your birthday, and when you beg your parents, adults in your life probably give you money. How can you follow Joseph's example and use this money wisely?

_____

_____

Genesis 47:17-19

17 *So they brought their livestock to Joseph, and he gave them food in exchange for their horses, their sheep and goats, their cattle and donkeys. And he brought them through that year with food in exchange for all their livestock.*
18 *When that year was over, they came to him the following year and said, "We cannot hide from our lord the fact that since our money is gone and our livestock belongs to you, there is nothing left for our lord except our bodies and our land.* **19** *Why should we perish before your eyes—we and our land as well? Buy us and our land in exchange for food, and we with our land will be in bondage to Pharaoh. Give us seed so that we may live and not die, and that the land may not become desolate."*

1. Joseph saw an opportunity and took advantage of it. He had something the people needed (food) and gave it to them for a small profit (animals.) This is called being an "entrepreneur." What skills or services can you provide for others?

_____

_____

_____

_____

2. If you had some extra money right now, what would you do with it?

_____

_____

3. Have you ever been desperate for something? Who helped you in your time of need?

_____

_____

_____

_____

Nehemiah 5: 1-5

1 *Now the men and their wives raised a great outcry against their Jewish brothers.* 2 *Some were saying, "We and our sons and daughters are numerous; in order for us to eat and stay alive, we must get grain."*

3 *Others were saying, "We are mortgaging our fields, our vineyards and our homes to get grain during the famine."*

4 *Still others were saying, "We have had to borrow money to pay the king's tax on our fields and vineyards.* 5 *Although we are of the same flesh and blood as our countrymen and though our sons are as good as theirs, yet we have to subject our sons and daughters to slavery. Some of our daughters have already been enslaved, but we are powerless, because our fields and our vineyards belong to others."*

1. Why did the people in this short story feel hopeless and frustrated? The most obvious reason is that they were hungry and had no grain. Can you find another reason?

_____

_____

_____

2. In Shakespeare's play "Hamlet," a father tells his son, "neither a borrower nor a lender be." Why might this have been good advice for Nehemiah's friends? Why is it good advice for you?

_____

_____

_____

3. How do you think the people in this story felt as the result of being enslaved to the people they borrowed money from? What are a few ways people become enslaved to those from whom they borrow money? How can you keep from falling into this trap?

_____

_____

2 Kings 5:13-17

13 *Naaman's servants went to him and said, "My father, if the prophet (Elisha) had told you to do some great thing, would you not have done it? How much more, then, when he tells you, 'Wash and be cleansed'!"* 14 *So he went down and dipped himself in the Jordan seven times, as the man of God (Elisha) had told him, and his flesh was restored and became clean like that of a young boy.* 15 *Then Naaman and all his attendants went back to the man of God. He stood before him and said, "Now I know that there is no God in all the world except in Israel. Please accept now a gift from your servant."* 16 *The prophet answered, "As surely as the LORD lives, whom I serve, I will not accept a thing." And even though Naaman urged him, he refused.* 17 *"If you will not," said Naaman, "please let me, your servant, be given as much earth as a pair of mules can carry, for your servant will never again make burnt offerings and sacrifices to any other god but the LORD.*

1. Why do you think Elisha refused to take Naamans money? What does this teach you about being generous? What might your generosity teach other people?

DAY 22

Leviticus 25:36-38

36 Do not take interest of any kind from him, but fear your God, so that your countryman may continue to live among you. 37 You must not lend him money at interest or sell him food at a profit. 38 I am the LORD your God, who brought you out of Egypt to give you the land of Canaan and to be your God.

1. When this scripture says not to "take interest of any kind from him," or "sell him food at a profit," the "him" it's talking about is any relative or friend who has run out of money and fallen into poverty. Why do you think this law commanded the Jews to give their poor friends and relatives money without interest and food without profit?

_____

_____

2. It is no coincidence that this law ends with God reminding the people that He is the one who once brought them out of Egypt and gave them the land they lived in. Why do you think God gave the people this reminder just after commanding them to take care of needy people?

_____

_____

3. Think of a time when you loaned a friend or relative some money and expected them to pay you back. Did you ever get your money back? How did you feel while you waited for your money? Did the loan help your relationship with the person or hurt it? Would it have been better to have not loaned the person your money, or to have given it without expecting to get anything back? Why?

_____

_____

_____

_____

Matthew 20:1-16

1 *"For the kingdom of heaven is like a landowner who went out early in the morning to hire men to work in his vineyard.* 2*He agreed to pay them a denarius for the day and sent them into his vineyard.*

3 *"About the third hour he went out and saw others standing in the marketplace doing nothing.* 4*He told them, 'You also go and work in my vineyard, and I will pay you whatever is right.'* 5*So they went.*

"He went out again about the sixth hour and the ninth hour and did the same thing. 6*About the eleventh hour he went out and found still others standing around. He asked them, 'Why have you been standing here all day long doing nothing?'*

7 *"'Because no one has hired us,' they answered.*

"He said to them, 'You also go and work in my vineyard.'

8 *"When evening came, the owner of the vineyard said to his foreman, 'Call the workers and pay them their wages, beginning with the last ones hired and going on to the first.'*

9 *"The workers who were hired about the eleventh hour came and each received a denarius.* 10*So when those came who were hired first, they expected to receive more. But each one of them also received a denarius.* 11*When they received it, they began to grumble against the landowner.* 12*'These men who were hired last worked only one hour,' they said, 'and you have made them equal to us who have borne the burden of the work and the heat of the day.'*

13 *"But he answered one of them, 'Friend, I am not being unfair to you. Didn't you agree to work for a denarius?* 14*Take your pay and go. I want to give the man who was hired last the same as I gave you.* 15*Don't I have the right to do what I want with my own money? Or are you envious because I am generous?'*

16 *"So the last will be first, and the first will be last."*

1. This parable teaches us a lesson about the generosity of God. It says that in the end, all who work for God will be rewarded equally. As you begin to search for jobs, there will be times when you will work very hard and be paid very little. What does this parable teach you about what your attitude should be in these situations?

_____

_____

_____

_____

2. In the story, the landowner hired people that he saw standing around in the marketplace doing nothing. He gave them an opportunity to work. What do you think this teaches about the value God places on working hard?

_____

_____

_____

_____

3. Is it better to work hard, regardless of what you are paid, or to decide how hard you'll work according to how much money your boss gives you? Which kind of employee do you think a boss like better, trusts more, and is more likely to recieve raises or promotions?

_____

_____

_____

_____

4. What do you think the phrase "the last will be first, and the first will be last" means? How does it apply to work and the attitude you show at your job?

_____

_____

_____

_____

Acts 4:32-37

32*All the believers were one in heart and mind. No one claimed that any of his possessions was his own, but they shared everything they had.* 33*With great power the apostles continued to testify to the resurrection of the Lord Jesus, and much grace was upon them all.* 34*There were no needy persons among them. For from time to time those who owned lands or houses sold them, brought the money from the sales* 35*and put it at the apostles' feet, and it was distributed to anyone as he had need.*
36*Joseph, a Levite from Cyprus, whom the apostles called Barnabas (which means Son of Encouragement),* 37*sold a field he owned and brought the money and put it at the apostles' feet.*

1.In the early church "no one claimed that any of his possessions was his own." What does this mean?

_____

_____

_____

2. Why did the people share everything they had? What do you think their motivation was for selling their land and giving the money to the needy?

_____

_____

_____

3. We still have needy people in our churches and in our communities. Have you ever seen someone sell their house and give the money to the church so that people in your town wouldn't be hungry or without a home? Why do you think we don't usually see this kind of generosity?

_____

_____

_____

Proverbs 28:26-27

26 *He who trusts in himself is a fool,*
   but he who walks in wisdom is kept safe.
27 *He who gives to the poor will lack nothing,*
   but he who closes his eyes to them receives many curses.

1. When this proverb says that "he who gives to the poor will lack nothing," do you think it means that people who give to the poor will automatically have all the money they need? Is giving to the poor a way of bribing God into filling your bank account? If not, what else might this sentence mean?

_____

_____

_____

2. Have you ever given money to a charity that helped the poor? Have you ever personally talked to a poor person, looked him/her in the eye, and handed him/her cash out of your pocket? If you have, how did these two ways of giving feel different? Which one did a better job of helping you appreciate what you have or of loving people who have less than you? Why? Which is a better way of helping the poor?

_____

_____

_____

3. The needy often get extra attention at Christmas and Thanksgiving, when the rest of our country is busy eating well and spending money on themselves. Why do we often "open our eyes" to the poor during certain times of the year and then "close our eyes to the poor" during others? How do you think the homeless and hungry feel in March or June when the "Angel Trees" are taken down and the canned food drives are over?

_____

_____

Acts 3:1-8

1*One day Peter and John were going up to the temple at the
time of prayer—at three in the afternoon.* 2*Now a man crippled
from birth was being carried to the temple gate called Beautiful,
where he was put every day to beg from those going into the
temple courts.* 3*When he saw Peter and John about to enter,
he asked them for money.* 4*Peter looked straight at him, as did
John. Then Peter said, "Look at us!"* 5*So the man gave them his
attention, expecting to get something from them.*
6*Then Peter said, "Silver or gold I do not have, but what I
have I give you. In the name of Jesus Christ of Nazareth, walk."*
7*Taking him by the right hand, he helped him up, and instantly
the man's feet and ankles became strong.* 8*He jumped to his
feet and began to walk. Then he went with them into the temple
courts, walking and jumping, and praising God.*

1. What do you think the man expected to get from Peter and
   John? What did he get instead?

2. How do you usually respond when a hungry or homeless
   person asks you for money?

3. The man in this story was thankful for what Peter and John
   did for him. Sometimes, however, the needy don't act thankful for our help when we give it. Do you think they should?
   Why would it be easier to give if they did? How does this
   expose our wrong motives for giving to the needy?

Matthew 6:1-4

1 *"Be careful not to do your 'acts of righteousness' before men, to be seen by them. If you do, you will have no reward from your Father in heaven.*

2 *"So when you give to the needy, do not announce it with trumpets, as the hypocrites do in the synagogues and on the streets, to be honored by men. I tell you the truth, they have received their reward in full.* 3*But when you give to the needy, do not let your left hand know what your right hand is doing,* 4*so that your giving may be in secret. Then your Father, who sees what is done in secret, will reward you."*

1. What does it mean to "not let your left hand know what your right hand is doing?" Why is it best for our giving to be done privately, without other people knowing what we have done?

_____

_____

_____

2. Make a list of at least five groups of people around the world who need either financial help or simply for the public to be aware of their situation or need.

_____

_____

_____

3. Celebrities are often very public about the charities they contribute to and the large amounts of money they give. Are these celebrities showing off their generosity or raising awareness for causes that need our help? How can we encourage other people to help with causes that are important to us without trying to make ourselves look better for being generous or compassionate?

_____

_____

Mark 12:41-44

41*Jesus sat down opposite the place where the offerings were put and watched the crowd putting their money into the temple treasury. Many rich people threw in large amounts.* 42*But a poor widow came and put in two very small copper coins, worth only a fraction of a penny.*
43*Calling his disciples to him, Jesus said, "I tell you the truth, this poor widow has put more into the treasury than all the others.* 44*They all gave out of their wealth; but she, out of her poverty, put in everything—all she had to live on."*

1. Are we responsible for how we give? What might this mean for you?

_____

_____

_____

_____

2. Why are gifts you have to sacrifice something for in order to buy more precious? Does a sacrificial gift mean more to the person giving the gift or to the person receiving the gift?

_____

_____

_____

_____

3. What can you sacrifice from your budget this month in order to give someone else something they need?

_____

_____

_____

_____

_____

Proverbs 11:23-25

23 *The desire of the righteous ends only in good,*
but the hope of the wicked only in wrath.
24 *One man gives freely, yet gains even more;*
another withholds unduly, but comes to poverty.
25 *A generous man will prosper;*
he who refreshes others will himself be refreshed.

1. A person who gives freely is not controlled by his/her money. How might this allow him/her to gain even more?

_____

_____

_____

_____

2. A person who does not give freely (who "withholds unduly") is probably controlled by his/her money. How might this cause him/her to come to poverty?

_____

_____

3. The proverb says that "he who refreshes others will himself be refreshed." Complete the following sentence five times with five different answers. In each sentence, put the same word in both the first and second blank. "When I give to people _____ , I feel _____ in return."

_____   _____

_____   _____

_____   _____

_____   _____

4. Look at the sentences you wrote for question #4. Do you think these sentences are true?

_____

_____

1 Peter 5:2,3

2Be shepherds of God's flock that is under your care, serving as overseers—not because you must, but because you are willing, as God wants you to be; not greedy for money, but eager to serve; 3not lording it over those entrusted to you, but being examples to the flock.

1. Who is "God's flock that is under your care?"

_____

_____

_____

_____

_____

2. Think of some examples of people (political leaders, spiritual leaders, celebrities, etc.) who have helped others simply because of the money or power they could receive in return. Even though their motives have been wrong, these leaders have still managed to help thousands of people. How do you think their work would have changed if these people had done their work out of love for other people rather than out of love for themselves?

_____

_____

_____

_____

3. What does it mean to be an "example to the flock?" How can you be a better example to others by the way you lead them?

_____

_____

_____

_____